Ma'Kai!
Where Are Your Glasses?

Written and Illustrated by
Minyon Patton

proving
press

Book Design & Production: Columbus Publishing Lab
www.ColumbusPublishingLab.com

Paperback ISBN: 978-1-63337-486-7
E-Book ISBN: 978-1-63337-487-4

Printed in the United States of America
13 5 7 9 10 8 6 4 2

Meet Ma'Kai, currently a 7th grader striving toward excellence. At a young age, Ma'Kai had to deal with bullies at school teasing him because of his glasses. Fast forward to the present. He is now comfortable in his signature frames, and all of his friends are asking their moms for glasses to wear as a fashion statement. His friends say glasses are cool!

Uplifting young kids about their glasses is now a part of his daily life. "Be inspiring to each other. You never know what people are going through," says Ma'Kai, "especially a kid that may be less fortunate."

Meet Ma'Kai. He is just like every other kid who loves to have fun. He goes to school, plays the drums, and loves basketball. There is only one problem—he needs eyeglasses but doesn't know it, and his bad eyesight tends to land him in some pretty hairy situations.

Ma'Kai was having trouble seeing the chalk-board and reading. Squinting while trying to read, he had to hold his book so close to his face to figure out words.

His friend Milla noticed he was struggling and encouraged him to talk to his parents. Despite Ma'Kai's repeated refrain of, "I can see just fine," Milla helped him a lot at school.

As time passed, things became blurry for Ma'Kai. His teacher contacted his parents and suggested an eye exam. Ma'Kai still protested, "I can see, honestly I can." His parents took him to visit the eye doctor.

This is how I
see
EVERYTHING
without my
glasses...

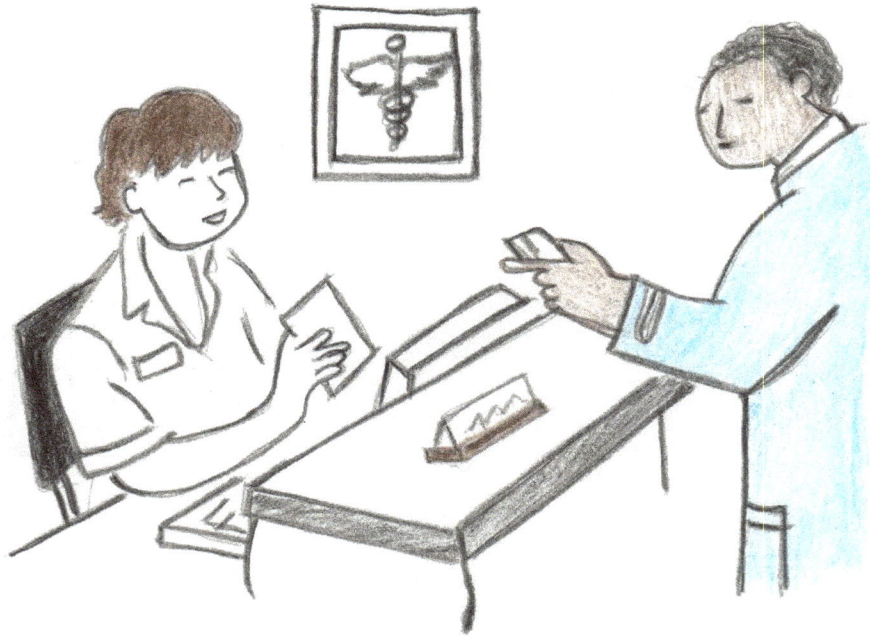

As they approached Dr. Mickey's office, Ma'Kai tried to make one last plea. "I can see," he said.

While Ma'Kai sat nervously in the room, a youthful Dr. Mickey entered and performed an eye exam. Turning to Ma'Kai once the exam was complete she said, "Young man, you need glasses to see properly."

Ma'Kai instantly had feelings of sadness, discomfort, and a fear of being different from other kids who didn't wear glasses.

Thoughts raced through his mind. He wondered how or when he would use his glasses for certain fun activities like swimming, playing on the playground, or even basketball—how uncomfortable!

But Ma'Kai's uneasiness quickly dissolved as he enjoyed a playful frame selection, and, most importantly, he ended up with perfect eyesight!

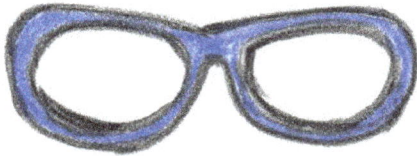

Nervous once he returned to school, he tried to hide on the playground to avoid being noticed.

One of his classmates, Jasmine, tried to encourage him to wear his glasses after he literally fell in the hallway and stumbled back to class in a daze.

Reluctantly, Ma'Kai put on his glasses when the teacher started writing on the chalkboard. To his surprise, she called on him to solve a math problem in front of the class.

His parade of predictable, dorky awkwardness had finally commenced. Ma'Kai's friends loved his new frames and they thought he looked so cool in them.

Ma'Kai's confidence soared, and he couldn't believe he had once risked his personal safety and comfort trying to hide his glasses.

Now comfortable in his new frames, he decided to make them his signature identifiers. They were not an ironic fashion statement but a life necessity.

Fast forward a year later. Now willingly wearing glasses, Ma'Kai is quite pleased with the way they frame his eyes. He gets compliments and he stands tall no matter what.

He's shed that silly insecurity, embraced his glasses, and encourages kids by letting them know glasses do not make you less attractive—they make you more capable of being the best you can be because you can see clearly.

So please, if you see a kid wearing glasses, don't make fun of them. Instead, encourage them, and let them know they look awesome!

About the Author

Growing up, my life was filled with adventure and wisdom. I was one of those lucky nerdy kids who was happiest tucked away in my room, a book propped against my pillow. Blocking out the real world, I was left free to enter the world of whatever book I was reading. Then to my surprise, I went from reading words to writing them.

Minyon S. Patton is the author of *Who Says I Can't be President? I Can Be Anything*, and *Ma'Kai! Where Are Your Glasses?* She is a construction engineer by day, and a novelist and serial entrepreneur by night.

Minyon is an Akron, Ohio, native, a mother of a young adult, and a granny to Ma'Kai who inspires her. She believes that an encouraging story can empower young people. For many of us getting glasses is a fun opportunity in accessorizing, but for children it can be traumatic.

When she is not writing, Minyon and her partner are managing their brands CharlieRue Collection/Works of Wonder or traveling the world. You can catch up with her at www.minyonpatton.com or www.charlieruecollection.com.

www.ingramcontent.com/pod-product-compliance
Lightning Source LLC
Chambersburg PA
CBHW041435040426
42452CB00023B/2987